From A Sky's View

a poetry collection

◊◊◊

Brandon L. Jackson

Printed in the United States of America

Brandon L. Jackson/Createspace, 2016

Cover Artist: Mark Crow

ISBN-13: 978-0692602225
Dallas, TX

www.brandonljackson.com

◇◇◇

Being strong just comes naturally to you,
that's why you love the hardest
And yes, being strong, gets tiring
but that's why you're an artist...
You give the best out of you

- The Strong Type

◊◊◊

To Randall Jones, a Lion of Judah.
A force among men
I miss you, friend.

Table of Contents

Author's Note & Acknowledgements

<u>Foreword</u>
Beyond Anything, Love Is With You

Poet **Brandon L. Jackson** has compiled a group of poems that are truly sincere and well-written. This book, *From A Sky's View,* holds poems that can be shared in any environment because they speak to the human experience in us all. Try as you might, you cannot get away from the work when the writer is committed to telling the truth about Love and Pain...Desire and Devotion.

These things stay on you.

In the poetry from this dreamer, the open-hearted one commits to penning responses to nightmares by pulling everything scary about the lies they tell and the secrets they hold. Brandon exposes these truths from microphone to the page.

We are all reflected.

If you open this book and you look for yourself, you will find that you are mentioned.

In a piece about *tears covering the day in you
when it rains*; poetry about *staying too long
with love and looking back to find yourself
better but indeed bruised somewhat by the
leaving.* There is a movement in and out of
love's chambers.

Self-sacrificing, self-preserving, selfless and
self-aware; beyond anything, Love is with you.
Through and through, Brandon's words
remind you to never forget about love. To
always remember to *feel* and *press hard*
against your pain until you can truly...

Smile on it.

-RonAmber Deloney, Poet

dreamers like you

Where do they make
dreamers like you,
who stay true to the Art of Life, despite
the bills overdue
Defiant
to all they say is "certain"
But soft with your belief
that ALL things
are possible
Lost in the remnants of vision
you dreamed up last night
that *shines*
from your hair follicles
Where do they make
dreamers like you,
too rooted to break or shed
So you left fear for dead but still
Beautifully wrote its eulogy
Womb full of regret and mistakes
but still gave birth to love songs
planted in tragedy
Strong roots, where do you stand in springtime?
Strange fruit, they hang and bury you
in the meantime
'Cause this was never supposed to be your season
As our blood blankets the streets

and poisons the ground
with reasons they say you shouldn't be dreamin'
And a faith that people feel
is just a waste to keep around
Where do they plant seeds like you?
'Cause it makes no sense to them
for you to choose to put food for thought
on pages
during hard days
when it's empty in your kitchen
Starving for something different...
For you to mention pain
that only peels into laughter
that heals
As if there was nothing left to cry over
I've tried my best to find
Snow angels in my winters
But after I was close to giving up
Choked by the ropes and linings
where I couldn't see the silver...
After my soul looked back and wondered
How on Earth I made it over...
I woke up floating on a cloud
Sent from one dreamer to another
Sitting beside forefathers with fire tongues
and skin the color of soil
Tangled in Love that saves
and Mothers who prayed
Who gave the Sun to their sons

when all the money went away, see
Dreamers like we are made
From everything torn down and ripped apart
When it was hard to believe in something
with so many weeds in the mind
and a desert in your heart
But somehow smiling like this, after crying like that
Sweetly nourishes the thirst
the hunger
the need
in growing good fruit to feed the souls of many
Especially in dark times like this
So where do they make dreamers like us, you ask?
Well if you trust in the answers
you can only *physically* see
Then you probably wouldn't even believe
A little ol' dreamer
like me

Part I

◇◇◇

Love Like Water

I appreciate
how you love me
like water
Covering and
Carrying me
through gray days
when rain comes
and I can't always be
as strong
as the Sun for you

soul runnin'

I'll be your "*sometimes*" now
until your "*always*" come
I can bring you sunshine now
'til your better days come
I just can't stay forever 'cause,
I don't know what
I'm runnin' from

This soul of mine
been runnin' too long
This cold of mine
don't stay warm too long
I wish I could build you something
but these hands
ain't always strong

This soul of mine
been used to climbing alone
because this world out here
won't promise you home
I try to keep from falling
but these legs
got my father's bones

A past like mine stay following me
Broken hearts like mine

leave no fight in me
You been trying
to love me Full
but sometimes love
runs you empty

soulmate theory

The best way to explain you
Is to start with how I've loved you
since Genesis
When the world was formless

You were the night
and I was born as the day
hiding behind horizons
'cause I was kind of shy in a way
Afraid to create something needed
and something new
You overshadowed my insecurities
to beautifully canvas me as someone Royal
Placed heaven on my head and smiled
as we painted the sky purple and red
Now they said,
Anything kept in the dark
shall come to the light,
How right they were
Because I wish to show you everything

The best way to explain you
is to continue with how I've needed you
in this Present
Where the world takes a form of
Heaven squeezed into material things,

Body temples torn into shambles,
Languages of hurt people
crying to deaf ears and blind eyes
that don't see everyone as equals
Got this love thing criminalized
As men plagiarize power,
steal credit from miracles,
publish only the images they see fit
and make them universal

Oh, what an existence it would be
if our lives spun on the axis
of Man's untrustworthy finger
On hands that destroy
more than they save
We are failures at being shepherds of one another
But somehow I was led to you

We be the day and night
Bodies wrapped tight in something God-like
but not perfect enough to stretch that far
And while the world failed to fill its voids
I danced in your stars
As I light you up, you cool me down
While you hold my arms to space
I keep your feet on the ground
The moon changes shapes, just like your smile
I love to see it full,
lighting darkness for miles

In all this Universe, I know it got lonely
Created from galaxy, but born on Earth
We be written like New Testaments
The evidence of History
Too solid for theories,
Too complex for evolutionary graphs
Despite this temporary science
We believe the spirit lasts
I know this because I've known you before
when Love was the Beginning
and we were just the aftermath

Faith ain't no fairy tale
and life after death ain't no superstition
because I've died many times
Resurrected in mercy that I didn't deserve
All to reassure me that there are reasons
For our living, our love and forgiving

You cover my tears
when the day in me rains
and when I've heard your night-cries,
I've dried your pain
What's constant in us, is constant in Time
So cool, calm and collected
Connecting your sunset with my sunrise
There are burning questions
of *"where the hell you been?"* in our eyes
But it wasn't my plan to make you wait

and it wasn't yours to be made patient
For destiny is never a human plan to begin with

They say opposites attract
and I guess we are no different
Because I forever feel young at heart
and your soul is ancient
So let's enjoy the moment
and never try to name it
Because soul

mates

just

are...

You don't need to explain it

places I've wasted time

If forever is for real
then you shouldn't
have to promise it...
People will say that *time heals*
But at times
you won't believe it...
In a life like this, it's natural
Wanting to return to all the places
to pick up the things you've wasted
But I've only time-traveled in dreams
Left trust behind eyes
I would've died for, I've
spilled full glass moments
under every class of moon
During sexual times when dark bedrooms
seemed to be the cure to lonely
'Cause this skin ain't always skilled
to know the difference
between the future it desperately wants
and the reality of the present it feels

I've abandoned minutes
of a simple forgiveness between these lips
Spit it out in fragments since,
I liked how pride tasted
and how anger completed my sentences

In a life like this, it's logical
Wanting to return to all the places
to pick up the things you've wasted
But I've overlooked new beginnings,
Held on too long to promises
you find out too late wasn't worth it,
Gave years to love
with no compass to unconditional,
While heartbreak takes seconds
in routine ways of how we stay the most patient
with things the most painful
Could've been successful
with all this potential by now,
where ideas were only left as ideas
and hopes that remained in the clouds

I know there are things we aren't proud of
And there may be longer days
of sacrificing passions
for bullshit like minimum wage
Loved ones spend decades in prisons
for systems that will never treat us the same
Weeks of second guessing dreams
the Creator didn't second guess giving you
while He was still putting you together
I've taken smiles for granted
Lost them in bad weather
Missing the warm seasons when the cold
Gives you all the reasons in this world to cry

That damn deadbeat Father Time...
He's always coming around just to leave again
But you'll learn that walking backwards
is not walking into second chances...
That's what the blind do
Who rather not see where they are going
Because the Truth is an acquired taste
For those of us tired of starving

If forever is for real
then you shouldn't have
to state the obvious...
People will say that *time heals*
But this is something
You'll have to experience...
'Cause like the church hymns say
Trouble Don't Last Always
Doors will close but windows open
For we got paths that were paved for us,
Revelations that will make you feel royal enough
With flaws that are centuries long
And a Love that paid for them millenniums ago
So with every opportunity
Tell him. Tell her.
I love you. I need you. I miss you.
I forgive you.
While we still have those chances to continue
Because in a life like this, it's understandable
Wishing to return to these places

Yet someone once told me
Nothing In This Life Is Wasted,
Only Recreated
We bury dead things to fertilize this soil
Growing up from winter lessons
when Spring brings us change
Because these roots are just as beautiful
As the petals that bloom only after the rain
And I must admit
I grow tall as ever, when something MOST HIGH
never seems to forget my
little ol' name
And when that same something believes
We can be so much better
Yes, we can still be so much better
Why else would yesterday recreate itself
in just 24 hours

smile

I never knew a smile
could be a dangerous thing
Until you made me do it, differently
There's electricity that stays around
Something that only the dead wires
in my bones can express,
about how elementary it is
for you to speak words
that give me air when I drown

I never knew it was this natural
To *SMILE*
and forget all of the things I wish to
Your heartbeat makes genuine sounds
that I'm not used to
Because the patterns of people that I move through
Are usually chaotic
broken
selfish
or confused

I never knew a smile could lead to questions
of greener grasses
on the other side of barricaded doors
Because the one I share my life with now
Doesn't make me smile

like that anymore
Now we used to be immaculate
Interpret each other in fifth elements
when we used to live in the stars
but when the questions got hard
The answers got silent
and we just don't *glow* anymore
Tired from forcing a potential
that doesn't wish to grow anymore
And while we hang onto the possibilities of a future
after the painful histories we've made...

I must confess
how much you've come along
and refreshed me

See, cheating is not in my character
but there's a nature of infidelity
in this smile I've been wearing
I come home, trying
to cover the smell of laughter we made,
hide the tears I laid on your shoulders,
shower away the penetration
of conversation we practiced, and act as if
I'm still committed to the one I share a bed with
I hope my thoughts don't think too loud
And that my kisses don't taste
like the words we've traded, I pray
my eyes don't hold pictures of the way

I've stared at you
Because since I've slept in the clouds again
Living on the ground is just not uplifting enough

I never knew a *smile* could be dangerous enough
To have me missing and meaning you
Wanting and needing you
Burning for and returning for
a restoration that hurt people search for
I've even started dreaming of you
when I know that I shouldn't
Beginning to write poetry for you
when I promised I wouldn't
I never was the kind to fly in social flocks
but you noticed me anyway
I never was the kind to give away broken hearts
but you noticed me anyway
I never was the first to speak, the loudest to preach
The wisest to teach, or the most interesting to meet
Yet you've come along
To try and complete me anyway

I never knew a smile could be
a dangerous thing
How it can make you feel fearless enough
to leave what's familiar
for possibilities
that cannot promise us *anything*
in return

silent rage of a hurricane heart

quiet storm, don't mourn no more
just cause he said he doesn't love you
and can't keep you warm no more
Convinced you to serve the godlessness in him
when he told you "I can't walk on water!"
Sent you messages in bottles
when apologies was all he had to offer
Left you empty and full with his children
Slept on pillows wet with questions
of *what could be wrong with you*?
instead of, *what's never been right in him*?

I write for you

Because I've seen the raging winds of deception
beat the tears out my mother
I've witnessed the waves of disaster
sweep the courage from my sister
quiet storm, don't mourn no more
just 'cause he said he couldn't stay
and be your Sun no more

The thirst in your eyes
makes you easier to drink
and the salt of his promises can't reach
the dreams he was the star of

or heal the wounds he's now a part of
I understand, you'd give your limbs for love
Especially when he'd travel
up shit creeks with no paddle
He spoke of safety in his bed of no harm
but when you were stranded in the middle of nowhere
how many times did he stretch out his arms?
As you struggled in bad weather
just to keep his levees strong

My, how time flies by
when you've loved someone loveless
for too long

So, quiet storm, no time to mourn no more
'cause I've seen the damages that rip through towns
and little girls' dream clouds
Through the neglect of fathers showing boys how
To honor and respect
the givers of life they learn to forget
Quiet storm, you'll continue to receive
what you continue to accept

See the world is like the ocean
and love is like the sand
where you'll have to swim to what you believe in
and sometimes drown to understand,
There are lessons at rock bottom
and silver linings that need you

Cloud carriers of peace, with real love to give you
For the more you are silent
Or the more that you rage
The more you tear yourself down
Trading loneliness for the embrace of his chains
It leaves behind generations of children
who grow up to believe
that they *must* deserve the same

So wipe the shipwrecks from your eyes
Because one time or many
we've all had our hearts broken into debris
but if the Most High thought we were just ashes,
the hundreds of second chances given
would've just been blown to sea, see
Greatness doesn't have to rush its growth
It comes naturally when the season is right
For you are ancient, Love
meant for a patient love
Something beautiful to sail in
Peace be still in blessings
where before you pray for a man
Meditate for *understanding*
For all the things that self-love can do
where destiny is written in the stars
as the universe looks up at you

So quiet storm
just 'cause he say

he "don't love you no more,"
Don't be torn apart...
He's just making room for someone
brave enough
whose love can calm
even a hurricane heart

manufactured man

I refuse to become
just some puppet for the majority...
So with heavy histories
in my bloodstream,
I block out programmed nightmares
of being placed in the ground
or in poverty
Because that is where they expected me...
I can feel their frustration in the air
I breathe it in the smog
I drink it in the water
I eat it in the food
Anything that their hands have touched...
I trust my prayers are strong enough
so the trees can carry them to Heaven's gate,
so the branches can serve my words on God's plate
before their trunks are cut down
Or maybe the breeze
can blow around my hopes and dreams
Before the Earth is worked ragged and to its bones
Can you feel their frustration in the air?
In the education I receive
In the generations I'll precede
In the police force that promises to protect me
In the long lines where time spills you
Until it's your turn to hear,

There's nothing I can do to help you
But, sir, my grandmother is crying
Left to lie dying at home
With medicine made by the high-paid ones
Prescribing expensive cures to *"low-waged scum"*
So I guess healing
will never come to us as fast...
I think they are frustrated
that this heart-engine
doesn't run off of expensive gas,
Or because they couldn't market
My passion for profit
They couldn't industrialize my culture
Or materialize my faith in God
Couldn't clone my aspirations
Couldn't murder my inspiration for poetry
Couldn't control me with double-A batteries
As I write FREE lyrics for FREE/DOM
See, I was made with love through a KING/DOM
And I think they are mad that
They couldn't poison our Wisdom
So they poison our air, our food, our water
and our children
Displace my revenue with overdue statements
where the payment
should've been my soul long ago,
But instead, I keep going to show
That we cannot be manufactured
By the standards of beasts in political clothing

Check my spiritual tags that say
Not made in America
Not made *OF THIS WORLD*
'Cause we come from higher plains...
Mustard seed grains that grow into
Bigger blessings/solutions
That won't always fit in the sight of humans
But I can feel change in the air
I drink it in the water and I eat it in the food
And I keep going for the love of children
Despite how I am the highlight
Of negative news
I refuse to bend
Because something eternal
Does not bow down or break
for men

pulse (smile prelude)

I felt your pulse this morning as you lay beside me
I didn't recognize its rhythm
I listened to your heartbeat as you slept beside me
But it didn't match with mine

Your walk is different
It's not inspired by my existence anymore
Your talk is different
The passion has taken another pattern

You don't do the things you used to do
You don't say the things you used to say
And I miss it so much but today
When I felt your pulse
and listened to your heartbeat
I couldn't help but think
Something has died

And as you lay beside me
I continue to think to myself
The reason why your pulse and heart feel so different
Is because they must be beating
for someone else

finally haiku

Future in your eyes
Your glance made me jump out of
A past that held me

kind eyes

you've got
kind eyes

The kind that we don't get to see
into that much these days
'cause it's been real cold outside...
No warmth
in those intentions disguised in sunshine
I've seen devils hide
in the same ones who say they'll pray for you
yet curse you LOUD in their closets
but you,
you got kind eyes
the kind of a prophet

Because somehow, I feel you know all my secrets
before I could even be honest and say
I don't know if I believe in love anymore
or miracles
or magic
Too many tragic stories of bullshit and bullets
that take down warriors with no War in them
Living in worlds where the size of your wallet
makes it easier to overlook
the content of your character, yes
Strange ain't nothing new here

but what's familiar in your stare?
Because somewhere along the line
I think we took the Supernatural out of love
and filled its belly with bricks
Gave our canvases to con artists
who can't paint Truth with brushes so
they draw lies with their lips
but you got the kind of pupils wide with
something safe and peaceful,
almost biblical enough to rest in and
dare you to leave your burdens,
A place where imperfections can feel
accepted again
I think I've seen that kind of genuine before
in the eyes of children
Before they know life isn't like what you pretend in
Doll houses or costumes
and that momma's kisses
don't always cover up the wounds

But you got kind eyes,
the kind that can see past these images

Deeper than the outer appearances
that we don't like to look behind
Blinded by pretty faces and strong bodies
that carry their disasters on the inside but
This heart ain't no perfect picture
Can't find the route to the soul

when the trail gets cold
but God must've placed His sunrise
in those eyes you smile with
The kind that we wish to find home in
more often

They blink poetry of how you've been
stripped down to nothing left
Kept daydreams on standby
and suffered through nights they haven't slept
They got your mother's scorn
and your father's storms in them
Like they've wanted to give up on hope before
Times like when I thought I
didn't believe in change no more

But life
gave you kind eyes

Reminded by tears that flow
and put out flames
under this skin when we grow
too much hate in our veins
and despite those bridges
lit on fire by mobs holding torches
of *I'LL BREAK YOU!* wishes,
There's something selfless
that I sense in you
I bet they never were expecting a quench of thirst

to come from the same eyes they left crying
or from the same heart they left hurt
Now I understand
Forgiving
is
more
than
one
action...

It's work

lost in someone else's dream

Have you ever
defeated the laws of physics
Lifted someone
to shake hands with God
Took on their ambition
as a fellow companion
Because the struggle is real
and the walk takes too long
Have you ever
added full-time passion
to fill their half-empty glasses
Made butterfly decisions
when you loved someone
out of their cocoon
because life should be about
transforming
about overflowing
and not some box that holds you captive
where you reach for the skies
but run out of room
See, you'd be the one
to break them free
So they could look into the mirror
and see the person
that you see

Have you ever lost yourself
in someone else's dream
being so far gone
that you couldn't even seem
to remember your own?

Have you ever
sown seeds in their hair
Left them there
and watered their wishes
Gave them all the riches you had
which wasn't much
Just a heart full of diamonds
that it traded like pennies for their thoughts
You know imagination does not
pay the bills
But you hoped that real love could armor them
Through the adversity
Through the doubt that cuts deeper
when dreams are slaughtered
by friends and family
But that wouldn't matter, because you'd be the one
to reassure them
To run barefoot through flower fields
and hot coals
Not worried about the next meal
because the soul is full of faith
and not of fear
that often looks to the hills,

and behind all of the smiles
is blood, sweat and tears

Have you ever lost yourself
in someone else's dream
being so far gone
that you couldn't even seem
to remember your own?

But you still push them further
Guide them onward
Help them be braver
Suffer a little longer this time
just to cross that finish line together
You stayed grounded
just to give them your wings
because you believed
in them
and they believed in you
when things felt so impossible
when things felt so unknown

But have you ever lost yourself
in someone else's dream
where the day that theirs finally came true
became the day that you'd wake up

Alone.

exhale

I've had trouble learning this again
How to take deep breaths
without the stress
of wondering what will happen
if I just let this go...
Everything that's been bottled up
that has stunted my growth,
everything that's turned my nights so blue
and my dreams into smoke

There's been feelings left in shadows
and words that have found their death
in the middle of my throat
There have been tears
turned into oceans
that I just refuse to spill
Heart explosions
I've concealed,
because hiding it all
doesn't make it real

Lately, I haven't felt this free
since there was a prison built
where my heart used to be
I've harbored memories
that have left me scared

I've swallowed poems
that I will never share
Locked secrets deep
and down below
The kind that I swore
Only God would ever know
yet still you stand here
and look at me no different
Expecting my life to be some kind of show
and tell

So excuse me one moment
while I exhale

...

Now I've told you
I'm no good with surrender
And I'm not used to the way
your arms shelter
this skin wrapped in thorns
You should run away
far away, if you're clever
But I'm confused at how you stay
and touch me like lover
but feel like friend
How many times have you been told
of all the things that do not glitter
Because I

am not gold
So stop treating me like treasure
and stop reaching to my soul
Because I am so afraid
that if I take you all in,
it means I must let it all go

So I'm learning how to do this again
How to breathe in before I choke
How to embrace the new face of Beginning
And how to breathe out with a hope
that I thought was dangerous
and that I couldn't take serious
Even though you've allowed me to breathe in
nothing but your patience
and a timelessness
that I've only found in the pages of books
in the kisses of grands and great-grands
in the songs where love is made
and in the brave look that says
you understand
Me
and I'm starting to tell
Because breathing didn't feel this *free*
Until I was able
to exhale

flawed love songs

My heart sang you before...

You came to me in
broken record dreams when
I was tired of repeating the same old thing
in my relationships
What captured me
was how I swayed in the jazz
that played from your laughter
Somehow, it made my past lighter
See, liars will smell
the vulnerability you wear
and will eat every piece of you
that was not left in your lap to share
But it amazed me
How I was willing to invest
in creating memories again
that had not promised me yet
How you suggested undressing my wounds
as if these marks were confused to be
Yesterday tunes of our souls,
when we were younger...
when music played...
and you didn't just hear it
You actually feared all of the Truth in it
Because I remember the ballads

from my mother's tears
And an addict's dance in daddy's hands
Where bad decisions teach you
about the beauty you deserve,
But as short as life is
It feels longer to learn

I swear my heart sang you before...
It hummed you in complete visions
of us paying homage to generations before us,
holding each other hostage in our rhythm
I dreamed of how I'd listen
to the blues you'd shout from your belly
As we'd cry poetry to our feet
How you'd make this pulse beat louder
than my nightmares
How I'd give you a freedom
that you were unprepared for
Because saying "I forgive you"
would be three of the hardest words
you'd ever speak
You'd give my imperfections a try
and I'd appreciate the way your patience
would bring a tear to my eye

We'd be everything my heart
Used to sing about
How one day, someone would bring about
Change

But unfortunately, you didn't bring
this melody with you
Because I've tried too hard
to listen for the sounds of love
being the way it could sing dead souls
back from the ground,
To breathe in a love
not filled with the pollution of doubt
I've tried
To supply wings to carry you to brighter clouds,
Drowned myself behind the floodgates
of the rage that buries you
I'm sorry I couldn't love you
past the broken
where hammer and nail couldn't seal
the disconnection
Hands swollen from the walls of protection we built
when we refused to fall again
Afraid of the intentions
behind someone else's touch
But my love, I am not enough to fix you
No matter how hard I've tried
to love such a scarred and burned victim
where the hurt hides deeper
than what you show on your face
Because I've traveled to that place with you
Inside the mistakes we've entered
and now from your embrace
that I've tried many times to escape

So who on Earth can fix these flaws?
Up late nights looking for beauty
and looking for God
In everything that's wrong
with this tragic way
we sing our love song
Are we *worth* fighting these odds?
Up late nights looking for peace
and looking for God
with this selfish way
that I stay here but you stay gone

We are flawed love songs
because if love is where God belongs
then all of this time...
We've been doing it wrong

more in me

The *more* in me
is what keeps the *more* in others
because givers give
until there is nothing left

The *more* in you
is what keeps the *more* in me
because Love restores everything
you give from yourself

Part II

◇◇◇

Love Like Lions

I appreciate
how you lead me
to love the history in your hair,
to taste the bravery in the roars
that our hearts make
Every time you take my hand
And we set Ego aside
to fight in these pride lands
with horizons to set our eyes on
Loving bold
and loving free
like lions

the noise

They say
he's nothing but the mistakes
of the generation before him
Body mapped in tattoos he uses
to cover up the pieces
of not knowing what Peace looks like
Defeat gets louder at night
where police sirens ring like
dinner bells
His kindred are caged in jail
So they can't join us at the table
Maybe that high will fly him far enough
with wings
to bring back angels
because too many are dying
Now he don't care that much for living
Rather stay in between her thighs
to make him forget what he's *feeling*
As the labels and conditions follow him
As the idea of blaming himself swallows him
'cause he hates to see his own face in his children
But I hear music in him
even though he's surrounded by the noise
of too many girls played like instruments
and too many tunes of self-destruction
in our boys

They hurt too much in silence
and can't find nothing to fill the void
So they just learn to deal this way

She say
being lonely gets too heavy sometimes
So she looks for change
in strange men
who say they can turn her tears into wine
Back then, her daddy was so proud
but since he's been gone
I mean, stolen
I mean, shot down...
Ain't no one left to refill the QUEEN in her steps
So the world drums insecurities loud enough
so the dogs that prowl
can smell them
She don't like the shade of her skin
so she cracks it open with syringes
Begging to be loved broken
'Cause sober love don't conquer all
and she doesn't like that pressure of standing
so she wears heels high enough
that make it easier to fall
But I hear music in her
Even though she's surrounded by the noise
of too much rhythm and blues in her eyes
Too much heavy metal in our boys
They hurt too much in the quiet

and can't find nothing to fill the void
So they just learn to love this way

They cross paths
after long days when the hurt got too bad
On dance floor altars,
they leave their burdens there
Then they dance in motel rooms
where they lick each other's wounds
and run for their lives
through each other's hair
They feel safe, 'cause they share in misdirection
The monsters they face, they don't see in each other
So he and she don't use protection

They just wear their skin loose,
Drag it far behind them
after life stretched it thin,
Can't tell the difference between their past
and their shadows
So they run around in the chaos
Looking to put some sunshine
in their sorrows
Begging someone to hear the music in them
To listen to the lyrics of broken spirit
that shouts loud from their throat
To listen for the notes of lost hope
where nonfiction melodies can depict them
As GODLY rhythms

And not the product of some godly wrath
That was just...man-made for them
So let your tongue be the tool to uproot mountains!
Where maybe we can find
all of the missing bravery,
The kind our history had
And all of the necessary vision,
the kind our futures will have...
To face what is beautiful
and recreate what's been destroyed
Because second chances sound like sunrise
and Love can fill the voids
Creating us to dance to the music of still living
instead of just trembling
to every beat of its noise

empty things

We are greater
than the dead weight we carry,
than those memories that swing heavy
on Yesterday playgrounds
where our hearts are trapped in patterns
because it keeps them safe and sound

We are greater than our past,
than our neighborhoods,
Taller than our fathers stood,
Greater than the average,
Than the baggage
that keeps our wings broken
from reaching mountaintop dreams,
Greater than the tears we cry
that steals the diamonds from our eyes,
Than the fear of what others might say,
Greater than any love that will not stay
The conqueror

We must remember the empty things
How lust expires and greed
won't make you rich with what you need
Today, anything meaningful doesn't seem
to be worth fighting for
Got these kids believing

That *senseless* things are worth dying for
but we are greater than your hurtful words,
Than the viral destruction
that just needs your screenname and password
We are greater than this mainstream beauty,
Than the pressures of being belonged to,
Than the misogyny we sing songs to,
Greater than this empty love
that our hearts beg to never leave
Because somehow we feel destitute
without the parts that make us grieve...
We are greater than empty politics
Greater than our empty pockets
Greater than a country's empty conscience
Where an empty justice believes
That it serves us by sacrificing human beings

I know you've been feeling homeless at heart
and incomplete in the soul
I know they say good things fall apart
and all that glitters ain't gold
I know you're upset, at how Time can disrespect you
when lonely leaves no back in your bone
WE know about the rocks and hard places!
The rain on rooftops
and unstable foundations
That left us empty handed on several occasions
But if letting it all go, became impossible to do
If life had no choices

then what would you hold onto?
'Cause I'd stretch these arms miles wide
to thank God that prayers don't die on ceilings
And embrace the dreams I've seen
hitchhiking for a place to go
This is for young women
Giving shoulder as shelter to the opinions
of *everyone* else
This is for young men
With fists burned by anger
Leaving behind the ashes of himself
I'd tell them, these arms weren't built
to fold people into boxes
And these hands that feed this mouth
Know that we cannot live by bread alone
And that our cup doesn't run "under"
We are greater than the empty things
That will get too heavy to hold onto

And here's what I've learned after
You let go of what takes you for granted
And hold onto the things that matter...

1. I am NOT my father
2. Hatred is a killer
3. To live is to sometimes suffer
4. Hurt is loud, karma is louder
5. Do not take what any snakes offer
6. Appreciate your elders

7. Love is in fact a conqueror

8. Move your words like water

9. Use them to part darkness like Red Seas

10. Connect them to the streams of another

11. You'll be attacked the closer you get to the purpose of the Creator

12. So I put my weight on prayers and paper

And I cannot promise that freedom
will ever be the easiest option
But it's enough to grab LIFE so tight
until we both shed tears and say
I will *never*
lose you
again

the strong type

Wish I was strong like some...
Like the ones who wear the soul sleeveless,
so no emotion ever sticks
Like those who can teach their hearts to beat
in empty languages that speak
alien to me
Or like those who can wash away
the stains of memory
that feel so *permanent* to me
Dreaming is a world for the weak
At least, that's what they told me
They tease boys for loving differently in school
Frequently murdered now whenever love
doesn't follow their rules...
Friends have said,
Don't go chasing reality behind someone's eyes
'Cause that's how they will use you
Don't go wishing on candles or shooting stars
'Cause that's how love will fool you

I used to believe I'd find someone to
Put meaning in my movement,
Give me music in my dreams
But deception wakes you up in mornings
after denial kept you warm at night
I used to be the optimistic type

Always wondering what heaven looked like
because something that is "heaven-sent"
should never be counterfeit, right?
I used to be the romantic kind
Trying to find silver linings around lying lips
that whispered, *we'll be okay*
because the clouds are where we slept
Superheroes by nature is what we called it
and Supernatural is how it felt

I wanted to be strong like them
who said, *Tough skin is the only protection*
against falling,
Who said, *This world is war*
And crying eyes aren't for black boys
who can't see clearly when walking into battle,
Who said, *the heart is the enemy*
when trying to heal from your past
So you better keep it quiet
because anything real, doesn't last...
So I built my walls high
'cause I started to believe them when
my All was never enough
I wanted to be strong and safe in
Learning not to care so much
So since then I've spread my oceans wide
and I've cut my losses loose
I've planted my mountains high and
I've walked in bigger shoes

I've now hurt some, who may have never
deserved it
Because I used to be weak for the ones
who were strong enough to hurt
on purpose
So now that you know this,
do you notice how strong they made me?
Now that you know this,
do you notice how long it takes me?
To be strong again when you're around
Giving me smiles that stretch
further than scars
And kisses that take the bitter from my mouth
I can't go back to being weak
or letting my guard down
I've never learned to deal with lonely
I've never liked the way it sounds

I used to be that brave, optimistic
romantic, poetically driven type
But when you've hurt for too long,
You start to work better alone
being closed up and strong
Yet you tell me, *It's okay*
to lay on your shoulder
and leave my colder thoughts there
You said, *being strong just comes naturally to you*
That's why you love the hardest
And yes, being strong gets tiring

But that's why you're an artist
You give the best out of you...
So cry when you need to
'cause the strong can get weak too
Brandon, you can cry when you need to
'cause the strong sometimes get weak too

So I cried
The moment you said you loved me
Because I feel strong enough
to believe you

nature haiku

Nature nurtured us
If plants need Sunshine AND Rain
I feel we're ready

no prejudice

When hearts break
they all sound the same
with beats that weep in different tongues
and a disappointment that speaks
in one language...
Evil intentions
are not wrapped in skin complexions
They hide freely in the hearts
of whoever invited them in

The innocent see heaven too early
'cause it's too much hell in being "different"
So mothers cry universal tears
when death segregates them from their children
Poured out from Golden rules
That we preach but never practice in our values

Heartache has no prejudice
It doesn't define us by opinion
or divide us into sections
It'll happen
when thieves think we are more attractive
in sadness
On days when real love seems unfamiliar
As hatred is passed between generations of strangers
Ignorant lips

bruise deep to the spirit
Because society said that she was too BLACK
Or they sentenced him to hell
Because he walks with a "switch",
Twisted the **I Am That I Am** in God's children
from burning bush to racial slurs,
Raised in the stench of broken promises
that equality would be delivered soon
As the heart and mind
fight for their independence
from those labels written
by historical wounds

But heartache has no prejudice
It'll come uninvited and will treat us all the same
Since the real rocket science
is the confusion in finding the roots of compassion
As we run in our brother's shoes
and stand in our mother's pain,
In a world where disease sees no color
but leaves its stigma in the water,
Where addiction finds us equals
Turning broken boys into broken men
Looking for dreams inside pipes
and genies inside bottles,
Where our girls can't find their worth
when called anything but beautiful
So darkness raped her rainbows
Colorblind of her potential

I once saw my reflection
in the face of a person, hurting deep like me
Our tears were salted by ocean
Skin molded by sand
Created by hands of the Most High
We shared battles that were bigger than our time
Inside wars not concerned about who gets killed
As long as we perpetuate
The lives lost and the blood spilled
But despite our ages and sexes, religions and faces
Despite our differences, followed by your judgments
I've witnessed the same pain and smiles
that travel between all of us
And while heartache has no prejudice,
Love is forever the universal language
So put it in control
YOUR LIFE IS NOT A CONSEQUENCE!
So live it, with all your soul
And while crying hurts sometimes
Our joy is so much stronger
No matter how different we may look or feel
In time, everyone's skin
Was made to heal

fell into each other

I never really
planned this thing
and I know
You weren't expecting me either
We just kind of
fell into each other
You tripped into my vulnerability
I stumbled into your desire
You collapsed into my loneliness
And I jumped into your fire

Multiple times we
Bonded our anatomies
Passionately breathing one another
Through moments promising forever
So somewhere along the way
We called it...*Love*
but we just kind of
Fell into this thing

I don't remember the process
of getting to know you
Or the contests of winning attention or affection
No long phone calls of intimate conversation
I don't remember you saying you'd die for me
I don't recall any first dates

Only late nights of *cooling* HEAT and
HEATING *cold*
I can't recollect promising to grow old
with you
What happened to being flirtatious?
The infatuation stages,
where I'd write your name on several pages
next to mine
Anxious for the time to hear you say,
"I've missed you"
Looking for the fireworks when I first kissed you
See, everything was skipped
to get to the explosions of sex we had
During our sad days

When I think of your touch
I should think of how my soul feels
Not just...my body
And when I'm alone I should feel
Sustained enough by something that's real
But somewhere along the way
We called this...*Love*
When really, we just fell into each other
And now we're left with "not enough"
Trying our best to *stand*
and finally
catch up

<u>almost</u>
(for the warriors fighting HIV & AIDS)

It's scary, the baggage I've carried
Where I *almost* forgot
the kind of bravery that momma taught
when she would say,
"Baby, fear and love will never look the same."
Still I was afraid to love myself
Because of all the mistakes I've made
The kind that people will engrave on your skin
where the more you wish to forget,
the more you start to wear them
Trying your best to undress
Exactly where all of the stigma begins

This back was *almost* broken
Bent over by the judgments that slept well
on my spine
Almost couldn't stomach the sight of my reflection
With faded dreams
That *almost* caved into the opinions
Of those who cast the first stones
but are too coward to remember
the rock bottoms of their own

See, I *almost* didn't hear
the poems in me.

It's scary, how naive we can be
Wishing to build houses
from words that promised shelter like we
could paint white picket fences
from the second chances we've given
Breathe...
in the passion that made us sweat
But we can't take the heat from kitchens
Holding the sharpest knives we've taken in the back
I've tried to find the right curtains
just to hide these tracks of tears,
Was almost heartless when this heart of mine
beat and said *This chest was not a home*
Almost let the feeling of alone define me
Used to envy those who could be so
Pyramid STRONG and brick-wall MIGHTY

See, I *almost* feared
all of this God in me.

Almost gave up when
I couldn't trade my story
for someone else's shoes
For someone who didn't track their blues
into every chapter
Almost lost my laughter
in the same water where my self-esteem
was somehow washed away upstream
Almost walked, like I was worthless

Almost forgot, that I was KING
Didn't know how much I could touch this world
that gave me no privilege
But you won't know about freedom
until you learn about forgiveness

Yes, I could tell you how much I was *almost* beaten
by the perception of others
Had *almost* forgotten the protection
Of prayers passed down
So I could make the ones before me proud
and teach by example to the ones after me
That no matter how low the clouds hang heavy
By your circumstance,
We are not slaves to the gravity
that holds us down
'Cause I *almost* forgot
the kind of bravery that momma taught
when I looked at myself and recognized Love
even after the fear came
Because like she said, fear and Love
will never look the same

So I'm here. We're all here.
Despite how life *almost* left us out
And we smile as we live and love on
Because *almost* still
Doesn't count

free spirit prayer

God, grant me the serenity to move
like a free spirit
With the bravery of a GIANT
Accepting the things I cannot change
between living and existing
Having the wisdom to know their difference
I wish to understand
Why we expect to find God's purpose
inside of situations that hurt us
Forgetting that pain,
was never a part of the Plan
I want the kind of wings
where there are no strings attached
But sometimes Heaven is a heavy goal to get to
when we try to fly
with feet on our back

I've loved in shackles
Crawled out from prison stories
where love didn't just hurt
It felt like it killed me in tidal waves
And even though I was raised by a Superwoman
You have to learn to be brave on your own, so
God and I have public conversations
inside of private prayers
Since I had a mother who worked to the bone

And a father who was never there

How do broken bodies
move like free spirits
when the scars are too wide
to find a healing place on this skin
that we've made tough?
I was taught to fill yourself up
With Christ-like love
And forgive even though you won't forget
But I've been closer to hate
more than I'd like to admit
So how do broken hearts
drum freedom
when damaged by those whose protection
was not enough?
And we lay next to the same weapons
We prayed to never form against us

I wish we could all move like free spirits
with the wind beneath our steps
and great action attached to our wings
Yet we become masters of opinion
and slaves to material things
Teacher, I want to be a Poet when I grow up
I want to feel alive in something a 9 to 5
can never give us
Lover, perfection is not something I owe you
But it was perfect timing in knowing you

Because after losing sleep
to experiences that will steal your peace,
You'll find out how faith has the muscle
to shake buildings
And how self-love will help you love
your enemies
Far from what we're supposed to be
But Something is for sure
That we're supposed to be...here

So how do free spirits move?
It's with love in the engine
And forgiveness as the fuel
By knowing there are reasons
in shedding skin, tears and words
From the moments when we prayed
Waited and listened
So pray, wait, and listen
Until you realize that you're worth more
than what was taken
And blessed enough to give back
what is given

So let's think like Freedom
Let's talk like Freedom
Let's move like Freedom
Because we're overdue for Freedom
With no room for fear
Because I know

I'm not what I'm supposed to be
But I know I'm supposed to be...
Here

these days

These days,
you can't only beware of the devil...
Gotta stay prepared to fight his advocates
This soul is not a window
to shatter by bullets
Or fracture by arrows they throw
to kill this heart we hope with, see
The poetry of poor folk dreams
gets painted across War scenes
Canvassed on street corners, prison walls
and caskets
No reparations can pay
for taking what is priceless
For single fairy GOD mothers who suffer
and worry after midnight
Working to make these kids graduates
Afraid to lose them under streetlights
The Truth
Comes gift-wrapped in our youth
That's how the Heavens send us signs
and the reasons why
they do their best to destroy us
Is because spiritually blind men
can't read between timelines
Or else they'd see
You don't need any fortune teller

to tell you how much power is in these palms
Where veins carry biblical strains
of all things beautiful and tragic
and when cut they bleed Psalms,
those David prayers of Love & Order
For knowledge is faithful
and ignorance is "once a cheater, always a cheater"
Our strength had no choice
but to stretch into oceans, because tears
Are saltwater teachers
Beware of evil doers
Dressed in uniform, who move like
Wolves torn from storybook pages
Who will speak in languages of change?
When we rather stay fluent in lies these days
But there is never any RIGHT in WRONG
Need more freedom songs in music
Check this movement
of bones that don't break
by any sticks, stones, or systems you create
See, this heart be made of Phoenix Ash
'cause it's a fire conqueror
Skin tells an Egyptian past
'cause we be Pyramid stronger
I bleed ancestor dreams
Sweat out plantation prayers
Protected by an armor
That you may never...ever...see
But I promise you, it's there

that's not love

You learn what love isn't
back in elementary school
Experience what love is
Sheltered back in mother's womb
But I've grown tired
of trying to find truths in tear streams
and bottomless apologies
that we've sunk ships with
Hell can't feel like Heaven
No matter how much you decorate it
I've drowned in empty beds
that stretch wider than Seven Seas
That haunts you
and scares the Peace from your dreams
Where lonely nightmares wake me up to ceilings
coldly staring back
Trying to love damages back on track
to beautiful things but see

That's not love.
That's not love.

You learn what love is
back in 1st Corinthians
when it was explained as something
Patient and kind

Experienced what love wasn't
back in adolescent days of infatuation
when something physical
made it easier to believe in miracles
But we're grown now
So the potential of what you could be
And the ugly reality of what you ARE
be the apples & oranges I keep in baskets
of hope
But this hope starves you
and leaves us fruitless
Lies carved from your throat can't feed this
Third World Country you let beat hunger
in my chest
Yes, making someone your Everything is an illness
if we simply love each other because
We both weren't complete to begin with

Because this is not love
that sings prison songs
that keeps heart leashed in chains
that holds my breath captive too long
Gasping for what's authentic
when the only real thing left I cry
and speak from my lips
and that falls to my lap
is the weight of your name

This is not love

that tears wing from birds
that destroys building with empty words
that keeps our needs dead silent
Excusing pain from how it hurts
When we just call it being "passionate"
When we are the drug addicts to goodbyes
To the *high*
of the lows we fold into
But darling, in the words of Maya Angelou
Love Liberates You
Because real love is *freedom*
and not some fairy tale that we just
get sold into

words less spoken

I've traveled roads not taken
Despite the loneliness in them
Learned lessons that were hidden
Despite how hard it was to find them
I've traveled in poems
not yet written,
I've hated and forgiven,
Loved what's correct
& loved what's mistaken
I've lived in fear
& I've lived like brave men
I speak the words less spoken
& pour out feelings
many are ashamed in
I speak for those
Who have felt less *human*
Less Angel
and even more so
Less chosen
The ones most broken
Can find the most God in them
So I say Ashe! Amen!
to giving everything from the heart
Even when the world
shows no interest
There's healing in those words less spoken
So use them when you're scared to,

when no one wants to listen,
when they turn you down
and bring their music up loud
because you don't speak to popular opinion
Be the voice for the voiceless
Use the gifts that you were given
Because there is power in your Truth
which makes all the difference

the older I get

Didn't you know there are stars
in my atoms
and oceans in my tears
These hands are not your bridges
just to give you a place to stand,
and even though you think
my kindness is weakness
The trust that I give
is not your promised land

The older I get
the more I understand
that there is no time to take love for granted
and that it's okay to cry
when I miss my friends,
The ones who've transitioned
into Light dimensions
where one day I might,
just see them again

The older I get
the more I realize there's no time for regret
I work harder in order to be greater
So that my mother can rest
I cherish the times when I was young
and the minds of little ones

where I can easily see myself

So you have to watch what you say
and believe in what you do
They may tear off my wings
but I keep Heaven on the shoulders
They may dig a grave for me
when we were always told by the elders
that "If you dig one ditch, you better dig two"
But the older I get
the more I'd write letters from the soil
and grow tall still
in forgiveness for you

The higher I go
the more my hunger longs
for things that are fruitful
Epically woven & historically written
to know my worth
and to know my limits
For my life is living proof
that we do exist as miracles

So the older I get
And the uglier this world becomes,
It doesn't take much anymore
To break down and set tears free
for *anything* that's done
Beautifully

Author's Note & Acknowledgements

I am grateful for this project and I thank God for the gifts granted when I was still just a soul floating around in His embrace. This is the third project where I have published my personal collection of poetry to share with the world after stepping over hurdles of my own insecurities, self-criticisms and fear. Although, as many times as I've tried to shake this urge of expression and was on the edge of just giving it up, reassurance comes in the most unexpected places. For this, I am thankful for transition. This dream of poetry and authorship has been beating inside me since tender ages and to now witness the growth between three collections, I am grateful and excited for what's to come. Each day is a blessing and if I am long gone tomorrow, hopefully I have left something behind to touch, move and inspire someone who desperately needed it. For this, I am grateful.

I feel that we go through life in our own stages, depending on the choices and on the hearts of the Individual. My first book, The

Parts Medicine Can't Reach, was a very emotional project that surrounded love experiences and mighty heartbreaks. As the journey of maturing continued, the second book entitled Somewhere Between Logic And Emotion was born from a place of finding my way out of confusion and into a more light-filled mindset of redefining self-worth and accountability for my actions. Now this current collection and labor of love, From A Sky's View, contains poetry that speaks from the beauty and struggles of a generation dealing with Time itself. In this stage, I wanted to share the anxieties I've felt inside of routine living and the unnecessary fear of running out of time before fulfilling that God-given purpose. It strongly deals with the mindset of how we treat ourselves and how we treat each other in this similar journey that we all share. It deals with the "What-Ifs" and the "Shoulda, Woulda, Coulda's" that we fret about in our relationships and in our everyday mission. It's about our frustrations with patience and different lessons of forgiveness. It's about the things we do see and also paying homage for those *unseen* things. I, too, wanted to shadow how cold we as people are becoming in a world where showing your truth and emotion is hardly deemed popular. At the end of the day, we all want to be fulfilled. To be loved. To not feel expendable. To have joy. And when those things aren't easily obtained or are stolen, we fear and become anxious questioning our abilities and our worth by the timeframe that we set in our own heads instead of that which is aligned with something Higher. However, after all of the living, loving, laughing and letting go of what keeps us from flying, one day we'll look down from a sky's view and finally think to ourselves...what were we so worried about?

Thank you God. Thank you Mama. Thank you to the grandparents and great grandparents I have and never knew. Thank you to my sister, Crystal. Thank you my friend, mentor and spiritual mother, B Randall. Thank you fellow artists who bleed from their hearts. Thank you RonAmber for your beautiful art, support and contributions to the people. Thank you Priscilla Rice. Thank you Calvin Sharp Jr. Thank you Lyn Lyric, my artistic kindred spirit. Thank you Ashley Wilkerson. Thank you Harold Steward. Thank you Kevin Anderson. Thank you

Vicki Meek. Thank you Rafael Tamayo. Thank you Mark Crow for an outstanding cover. Thank you Kijana Martin for your art and knowledge. Thank you to my friends and supporters. Thank you Kristina Walsh. Thank you Narsha Wilson. Thank you Ashley Culpepper. Thank you Randall Jones, Rest In Paradise. Thank you Giselle Robinson, Rest In Paradise. Thank you Heart & Soul. Thank you Queerly Speaking. Thank you The Truth Project. Thank you Verse & Rhythm. Thank you Poetry Smash Series. Thank you listeners. Thank you readers. You are loved. You are Love.